T0142675

The Tickle Thumbs

A Ticklish Counting Book

CHRIS BOWERS

Archway Publishing books may be ordered through booksellers or by contacting:

Archway Publishing
1663 Liberty Drive
Bloomington, IN 47403
www.archwaypublishing.com
1 (888) 242-5904

ISBN: 978-1-4808-8150-1 (sc)
ISBN: 978-1-4808-8151-8 (hc)
ISBN: 978-1-4808-8152-5 (e)

Print information available on the last page.

Archway Publishing rev. date: 9/19/2019

Tucker is a Brittany Spaniel who has brought lots of laughs to our family.
Help Tucker find the Tickle Thumbs!

1,2...

Someone is coming for you!

3,4...

Who is knocking

at your door?

5,6...

They are full of tricks!

7,8...

I hope they do not wait!

9,10...
Hooray!
It's them!

FEE, FI
FO, FUM,

Here come the...

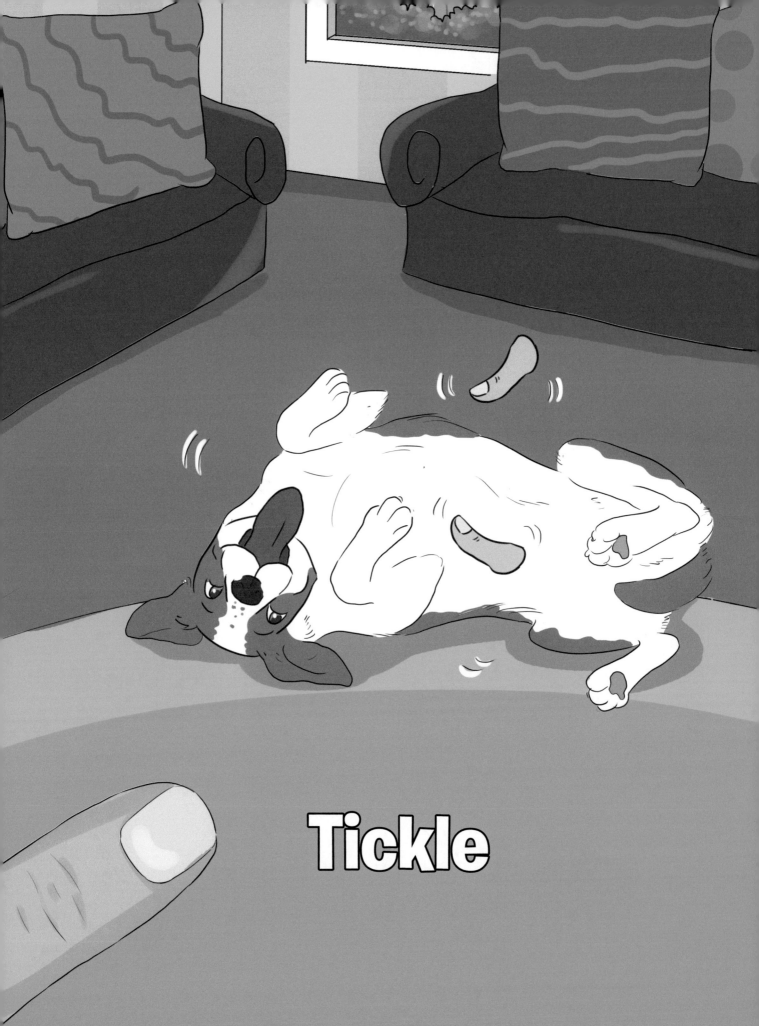

Tickle

Thumbs!!!

Let's count again!

About the Author

Chris Bowers is a husband and father of two sons. Over the years he's enjoyed telling stories to his children, and came up with the idea of the Tickle Thumbs. He hopes you have lots of laughs counting with your children.

Printed in the United States
By Bookmasters